the everyman series

being God's man...
in leading a family

Real Men. Real Life. Powerful Truth.

Stephen Arterburn

Kenny Luck & Todd Wendorff

WATERBROOK
PRESS

BEING GOD'S MAN...IN LEADING A FAMILY
PUBLISHED BY WATERBROOK PRESS
2375 Telstar Drive, Suite 160
Colorado Springs, Colorado 80920
A division of Random House, Inc.

All Scripture quotations, unless otherwise indicated, are taken from the *Holy Bible, New International Version®*. NIV®. Copyright © 1973, 1978, 1984 by International Bible Society. Used by permission of Zondervan Publishing House. All rights reserved. Scripture quotations marked (NASB) are taken from the *New American Standard Bible®*. (NASB). © Copyright The Lockman Foundation 1960, 1962, 1963, 1968, 1971, 1972, 1973, 1975, 1977, 1995. Used by permission. (www. Lockman.org).

ISBN 1-57856-682-7

Printed in the United States of America
2003—First Edition

10 9 8 7 6 5 4 3 2 1

contents

welcome to the every man
Bible study series

As Christian men, we crave true-to-life, honest, and revealing Bible
study curricula that will equip us for the battles that rage in our lives.
We are looking for resources that will get us into our Bibles in the
context of mutually accountable relationships with other men. But
like superheroes who wear masks and work hard to conceal their true
identities, most of us find ourselves isolated and working alone on
the major issues we face. Many of us present a carefully designed
public self, while hiding our private self from view. This is not God's
plan for us.

Let's face it. We all have trouble being honest with ourselves, particularly in front of other men.

As developers of a men's ministry, we believe that many of the
problems among Christian men today are direct consequences of
an inability to practice biblical openness—being honest about our
struggles, questions, and temptations—and to connect with one
another. Our external lives may be in order, but storms of unprocessed
conflict, loss, and fear are eroding our resolve to maintain integrity.
Sadly, hurting Christian men are flocking to unhealthy avenues of
relief instead of turning to God's Word and to one another.

We believe the solution to this problem lies in creating opportunities for meaningful relationships among men. That's why we

designed this Bible study series to be thoroughly interactive. When a man practices biblical openness with other men, he moves from secrecy to candor, from isolation to connection, and from pretense to authenticity.

Kenny and Todd developed the study sessions at Saddleback Church in Lake Forest, California, where they teach the men's morning Bible studies. There, men hear an outline of the Bible passage, read the verses together, and then answer a group discussion question at their small-group tables. The teaching pastor then facilitates further discussion within the larger group.

This approach is a huge success for many reasons, but the key is that, deep down, men really do want close friendships with other guys. We don't enjoy living on the barren islands of our own secret struggles. However, many men choose to process life, relationships, and pressures individually because they fear the vulnerability required in small-group gatherings. *Suppose someone sees behind my carefully constructed image? Suppose I encounter rejection after revealing one of my worst sins?* Men willingly take risks in business and the stock market, sports and recreation, but we do not easily risk our inner lives.

Many church ministries are now helping men win this battle, providing them with opportunities to experience Christian male companionship centered in God's Word. This study series aims to supplement and expand that good work around the country. If these lessons successfully reach you, then they will also reach every relationship and domain that you influence. That is our heartfelt prayer for every man in your group.

how to use this study guide

As you prepare for each session, first review the **Key Verse** and **Goals for Growth,** which reveal the focus of the study at hand. Discuss as a group whether or not you will commit to memorizing the Key Verse for each session. The **Head Start** section then explains why these goals are necessary and worthwhile. Each member of your small group should complete the **Connect with the Word** section *before* the small-group sessions. Consider this section to be your personal Bible study for the week. This will ensure that everyone has spent some time interacting with the biblical texts for that session and is prepared to share responses and personal applications. (You may want to mark or highlight any questions that were difficult or particularly meaningful, so you can focus on those during the group discussion.)

When you gather in your small group, you'll begin by reading aloud the **Head Start** section to remind everyone of the focus for the current session. The leader will then invite the group to share any questions, concerns, insights, or comments arising from their personal Bible study during the past week. If your group is large, consider breaking into subgroups of three or four people (no more than six) at this time.

Next get into **Connect with the Group,** starting with the **Group Opener.** These openers are designed to get at the heart of each week's lesson. They focus on how the men in your group relate to the passage and topic you are about to discuss. The group leader will read the opener for that week's session aloud and then facilitate interaction on the **Discussion Questions** that follow. (Remember: Not everyone has to offer an answer for every question.)

Leave time after your discussion to complete the **Standing Strong** exercises, which challenge each man to consider, *What's my next move?* As you openly express your thoughts to the group, you'll be able to hold one another accountable to reach for your goals.

Finally, close in **prayer,** either in your subgroups or in the larger group. You may want to use this time to reflect on and respond to what God has done in your group during the session. Also invite group members to share their personal joys and concerns, and use this as "grist" for your prayer time together.

By way of review, each lesson is divided into the following sections:

To be read or completed *before* the small-group session:
- **Key Verse**
- **Goals for Growth**
- **Head Start**
- **Connect with the Word** (home Bible study: 30-40 minutes)

To be completed *during* the small-group session:
- Read aloud the **Head Start** section (5 minutes)
- Discuss personal reaction to **Connect with the Word** (10 minutes)
- **Connect with the Group** (includes the **Group Opener** and discussion of the heart of the lesson: 30-40 minutes)
- **Standing Strong** (includes having one person pray for the group; challenges each man to take action: 20 minutes)

more than a provider

Being a good husband and father is not easy. In fact, for many of us, it is easier to build a career than it is to build solid relationships in the home. Some of us are all thumbs when it comes to our families. And when we look at the alarming statistics on marriage and family, we see too many men jumping ship, abandoning the challenge, and destroying relationships in the process.

When it comes to relationships with our wives and kids, many of us feel like the fool whom King Solomon described in Proverbs: "As a dog returns to his vomit, so a fool repeats his folly" (26:11). The fool was helpless to change because his character impeded his progress. Like him, we keep stepping in it and are at a loss to stop the cycle. We keep giving ourselves bloody noses by the choices we make, the words we speak, and the priorities we defend in the name of "needing a break." Most men know intuitively that there is a better way to do family life, but they just can't seem to execute the personal change required to make it happen. Over time most men are tempted to give up or bail out—and some men do just that. Maybe that's why you've taken the risk to explore this study.

The reality is that a struggling family man doesn't need a new wife, new kids, new diversions, or more money to resolve his family issues. He needs a new heart. The heart is the engine that drives character and fuels our interactions in the family. That's why the Bible tells us: "Guard your heart, for it is the wellspring of life" (Proverbs 4:23)—a healthy life for your family.

When a man feeds his heart with God's Word and takes steps to order his life around God's purposes, the ones who benefit the most are those closest to him. When I, as the chief influencer of my family, change, all the relationships and dynamics in my family change as well.

Our wives and children find it easier to connect with men they respect. And we gain that respect by becoming godly men who live out God's purposes in front of our families. This is the first step in changing the way things look and feel in the home.

Next, we need to look closely at the relationships in our homes and clearly identify God's purposes for us in those relationships. Finally, we need to look at the practical ways to build a family environment that is strong enough to withstand the inevitable chaos and conflict all families experience.

The dynamics of family life mold each of us into who we are as men. Just think about your own family of origin for a moment and consider how it has impacted you to this day—for better or for worse. If you let it sink in, you realize that the responsibility of leading a family is overwhelming. So much is at stake. The good news for each of us is that God has committed Himself to being our partner as we seek to lead our families. Our part is to seek out His direction for us in His Word, ask for His power to implement the changes we need to make, and take the practical, and sometimes difficult, steps

He calls us to take. Your family feeds off your leadership. It is the high honor of God's man to see that they get the godly leadership they need.

Our goal in this study is to stimulate personal reflection and honest dialogue with God and with other men about these matters. As you work through each session, look in the mirror at your own life and ask yourself some hard questions. Whether you are doing this study individually or in a group, realize that complete honesty with yourself, with God, and with others will produce the greatest results.

Our prayer is that you will be moved to embrace God's plan for your family and that you will experience His blessings as you risk going deeper in your faith.

own it

Take Ownership of Your Spiritual Journey

Key Verse

Fight the good fight of the faith. Take hold of the eternal life to which you were called when you made your good confession in the presence of many witnesses. (1 Timothy 6:12)

Goals for Growth

- Take responsibility for our own spiritual growth.
- Commit to pursuing God's purposes for our lives.
- Live out our faith daily in front of our families.

Head Start

In his landmark study on Christianity in America, George Barna pulled back the sheets and exposed men to a painfully embarrassing fact: Women are the backbone of spiritual life in America. Here are a few facts that really smarted. Women are

- one hundred percent more likely to be involved in a discipleship program at church;
- fifty-four percent more likely to be in a small group that meets regularly for Bible study, prayer, or fellowship;
- forty-six percent more likely to spiritually mentor someone else;
- thirty-nine percent more likely to spend time alone reading the Bible or praying; and
- twenty-nine percent more likely to share their faith with others.

Commenting on the story these statistics tell, Barna reflected, "Women, more often than not, take the lead role in the spiritual life of the family. Women typically emerge as the primary—or only—spiritual mentor and role model for family members. And that puts a tremendous burden on wives and mothers."[1] Say it with us, guys—"OUCH!"

As Kenny and I (Todd) minister to men, we end up talking with a lot of frustrated wives who have had to step up to fill the spiritual gap in their families. We've seen firsthand the negative consequences of this inversion of spiritual leadership in the family. Most tragically,

---

1. From "Women Are the Backbone of the Christian Congregations in America," 6 March 2000, Barna Research Group Online, www.barna.org, Ventura, CA 93003. Used by permission.

we see that the more leadership women assume in spiritual matters in the home, the more spiritually isolated men become.

We have been spiritually emasculated, and having given over our mantle of leadership to our wives, we have distanced ourselves from the center of spiritual life in our families. Even if a man wants to grow spiritually, he may end up doing nothing because it's "her" thing. And if he does pursue God in a tangible way, it might be considered as losing the argument or conceding defeat. Most men are too prideful and stubborn to concede that their wives were right.

Another by-product of this male spiritual malaise is that wives who are either unsure or unconvinced of their hubby's spiritual commitment may end up nagging their men to grow spiritually. We know of one wife who wanted her husband to read a certain book, so she taped it to the inside of the toilet lid! This woman is crying out: "I need you to step up!" Most men are surprised to learn that their wives long for them to step up and lead.

Barna summed up both the dilemma and the solution when he concluded, "If the Church is going to stem the tide of spiritual illiteracy and waning commitment to the Christian faith, men will have to reestablish themselves as partners and leaders of the spiritual functions of families."[2]

Well, what are we going to do about it, fellas? What are we going

---

2. From "Women Are the Backbone of the Christian Congregations in America," 6 March 2000, Barna Research Group Online, www.barna.org, Ventura, CA 93003. Used by permission.

to tell God when our days on earth are over and we stand face-to-face with the One who made us stewards of our families? One thing is sure, God's not going to buy the lame excuses we tell ourselves— especially when He's offered to help us in every way. The old cliché "You can't give away what you don't have" is especially true when it comes to spiritual leadership in the family. So the first step to being God's man in the family is simple: We must personally own our spiritual lives. What does that mean?

Connect with the Word

Read 1 Timothy 6:10-16.

1. What caused certain men to wander from the truth (verse 10)?

2. What contrast did Paul make between these men and Timothy, the "man of God"?

3. What do the two commands in verse 11 imply about our spiritual lives?

4. Which command stands out to you personally? Why?

5. What does verse 12 reveal about spiritual growth?

6. Why did Paul ask Timothy to look back to the time he first committed his life to Christ? What impact do you think that reflection had on his spiritual growth?

7. What do we learn from Jesus' example about taking ownership of our faith in God (verse 13)? (See John 18:33-37.) What did taking this stance involve for Jesus?

8. In what ways do you think Jesus' example helped Timothy sustain his motivation to be God's man rather than settling for a lesser commitment?

9. Does the promise of one day seeing Jesus Christ face-to-face increase your motivation to be God's man (verse 14)? Explain.

Connect with the Group

Group Opener

Read the group opener aloud and discuss the questions that follow. (Suggestion: As you begin your group discussion time in each of the following sessions, consider forming smaller groups of three to six men. This will allow more time for discussion and give everyone an opportunity to share their thoughts and struggles.)

I [Kenny] remember sitting in a Dallas hotel room, staring at a picture of my little daughter, Cara, and thinking about the journal I was trying to keep for her because I was traveling so much. It was 9 P.M. and I was still in my business suit. I had been traveling Monday through Friday for the past five months. My company had acquired our competitor, and I was part of the new operations team. I enjoyed being part of a merger because that was where the action was, but my role required me to commute to Dallas during the week and come home to Southern California on weekends.

Deep down, I knew that all my traveling was hurting my relationship with Chrissy and my first child, Cara. And it hurt *me* to miss so many precious moments with my new bride and so many firsts with my new baby. On the other hand, I was now solidly on the inside of the senior management team—something for which I had worked very hard. Nonetheless, after gazing down at my empty journal, I knew what I had to do. I took a deep breath and dialed the executive vice president.

"I can't do this anymore," I said into the phone while the VP listened to me talk about how much I missed my family.

"Okay, let's meet for lunch tomorrow and talk about it," he said.

All the next morning, I regretted making that call. *Maybe you're just tired,* I thought. *Maybe the pressure is getting to you.*

But I knew I had to pull the plug on Dallas. Over lunch, my boss listened to my desire to get back to Southern California. After some reflection—he didn't try to talk me out of my decision—he said the company could accommodate my desire to be closer to home. In fact, he believed he could find me a new contract to manage in Southern California.

What should have felt like a huge burden lifted from my shoulders, however, felt like a huge demotion. *Hit the showers, Luck. You're through with this company. They're sending you to the bush leagues.* Although I felt awful, deep down I knew that God was asking me to put my marriage and family first.

Gulp. I had to believe that.[3]

---

3. Stephen Arterburn and Kenny Luck, *Every Man, God's Man* (Colorado Springs: WaterBrook Press, 2003), 116-7.

Discussion Questions

a. Do you think I (Kenny) did the right thing? Why, or why not?

b. When have you faced a similar situation? What did you do? What role did your faith play as events unfolded?

c. In what ways is the pursuit of wealth or a preoccupation with your job presenting a challenge to your spiritual growth these days?

d. In what ways do the challenges listed in 1 Timothy 6:10 negatively impact your ability to be the spiritual leader in your family?

e. In verses 13 and 14, Paul charged Timothy to keep Christ at the center of his life. Who is charging you to do the same?

f. Based on this week's lesson, what specific steps will you take to facilitate spiritual growth in your life?

Standing Strong

At your funeral, how would you like your wife and children to remember you? Write down a few statements.

What can you do today to increase the likelihood that you'll be remembered this way?

Write a prayer to God expressing your desire to take charge of your spiritual journey. Read the prayer aloud to the group.

show it

Model Your Relationship with God for Your Kids

Key Verse

You know that we dealt with each of you as a father deals with his own children, encouraging, comforting and urging you to live lives worthy of God, who calls you into his kingdom and glory. (1 Thessalonians 2:11-12)

Goals for Growth

- Commit to thinking about life from an eternal perspective.
- Openly model the spiritual growth process to our families.
- Bring our experience with God directly into our relationships.

Head Start

Kenny and I (Todd) had totally different kinds of fathers growing up. Kenny's father was distant, protective, and unconnected. My father was engaged, involved, and encouraging. Both of our fathers were good men and good providers, but neither provided much of a deep spiritual example to follow. In both our families, we were left to figure out our faith on our own. Don't get us wrong! We both love and respect our dads. (Kenny's beloved dad passed away while we were writing this curriculum. He had met the Lord later in his life.) They're our heroes and we've told them so. But at the same time, we recognize that they didn't model the kind of spirituality we needed to see growing up.

What was your home like when you were growing up? Did you have a model to follow? What kind of model? Whether or not we realize it, we all had models in our families of origin. Most men model both good and bad character traits for their kids. But what kind of spiritual traits do we model in our families? The apostle Paul was a spiritual father to many. He modeled his faith among those whom he considered to be his spiritual children.

Whether or not we realize it, we are sending significant spiritual signals to our families. Our kids learn from us and imitate us! For example, Kenny's kids are avid UCLA fans. My kids have a passion for water-skiing. Why? Because we as dads have modeled an enthusiasm and excitement for college football and water sports. Why would it be any different in our spiritual lives? If we model a passion and enthusiasm for God, our kids will pick up on this. If we are Sunday Christians and God has no place in our lives from Monday through Saturday, then our kids will pick up on that, too. And if the Bible has no place in our lives, our kids won't learn from us how to hunger and thirst for righteousness.

The fact is, we model what we value. As our children watch our lives, they may wonder, *Does God really matter to Dad?* For our wives and kids, our actions speak louder than our words. We want our kids to grow spiritually, but are we modeling that growth in our own lives? If we do not offer a healthy spiritual model, the world will be all too eager to fill the void.

Connect with the Word

Read 1 Thessalonians 1:4-7.

1. What made the gospel real among the Thessalonians?

2. What did Paul do that proved to be successful (verse 5)? How did the Thessalonians respond (verses 6 and 7)?

3. How does this passage relate to your responsibility to model your faith in the home?

4. In what areas of your life are you doing well as a model for your family? In what areas do you need to improve?

Read 1 Thessalonians 2:10-12.

5. What characterized Paul's witness to the Thessalonians?

6. What, specifically, did Paul do among them?

7. Why did Paul use the father image to describe how he modeled his faith among the Thessalonians? What was the desired outcome of his nurturing and encouragement?

8. In what ways would you like to follow Paul's example in your family relationships?

Connect with the Group

Group Opener
What kind of role model did you have in your home as a child? If you are comfortable doing so, share a story about your relationship with your dad. Talk about the effect this relationship still has on you today.

Discussion Questions
a. Even if you did not have a good spiritual role model in your home, what did you learn from these Scripture passages that you can apply to your own family?

b. For what actions will *you* be held personally responsible?

c. What are you doing spiritually that you would like to see your children imitate in their lives?

d. What can you do to comfort, encourage, and exhort your kids? Be specific.

Standing Strong

What will you do this week to model something of spiritual worth that your family can imitate? Share with the group what you are going to do.

lead her

Follow God's Plan for Your Marriage

Key Verse

The LORD God said, "It is not good for the man to be alone. I will make a helper suitable for him." (Genesis 2:18)

Goals for Growth

- Take responsibility for leadership in our marriages.
- See our wives as the gifts from God that they are.
- Defend our marriages against Satan's attacks.

Head Start

Sin causes the friction that harms our relationships with others. Marriage relationships are no exception. Take two of the most godly, mature, absolutely wonderful, and nearly perfect individuals, put them under the same roof, and...*watch out!* Sparks start flying, trash cans get bashed in, doors get slammed, tempers rise, and the cat learns to fly—reluctantly. In addition, husbands go without dinner and sleep on the couch. Yet, in the midst of real life, God calls men to do more than just "hang in there." He calls us to be the spiritual leaders of our homes.

You might say, "Well, you don't know my situation." If it involves you, we know enough. Yes, it takes two to tango, but it takes one to lead. And marriage is more than a dance.

In God's original design, a husband was to be the leader, not the follower. But these days, too many men follow their wives instead of lovingly leading them. When God brought Eve to Adam, He expected Adam to lead in the relationship. How? As a tyrant? a dictator? a superior? No. Adam was to gently lead Eve, treating her as his helpmate—someone to share his life with. He was to give her strength and keep her free from danger as they both fulfilled God's plan for them in the garden. That's spiritual leadership. But it doesn't happen without a few setbacks.

Along with the joy and fulfillment we experience in being husbands and fathers, there is also pain and frustration. We love our role and we hate it. We want intimacy with our wives, close connections with our kids, and a tranquil home life. Yet, we sometimes struggle with the personal sacrifice it takes. Our good friend Paul offers us no comfort. He likes to say in his best *semper fi* voice, "Pain is the sign of weakness leaving your body."

If we are to become the loving husbands and spiritually nurturing fathers God expects us to be, we have to die to ourselves. This takes courage and, above all, character. Anyone not up for the challenge is a poser, a guy who says he is doing something but can't prove it. Some men are just selfish enough to think they can be a Ray Barone from the comedy series *Everybody Loves Raymond.* He's funny, but he's a failure. Laugh at him; don't imitate him. He's following the wrong blueprint. On the other hand, way back in Genesis, God gave us the right blueprint for how to lead in marriage.

Connect with the Word

Read Genesis 2:18-25.

1. According to this passage, how does God want us to view our wives? (*Note:* Notice the progression of thought: man was alone [verse 18], he had no helper/ally [verse 20], and God created woman and brought her to man [verse 22].)

2. Is your view of your wife in line with God's standard? Explain.

3. How should knowing that God is the One who "brought" you your wife help you accept her as a gift and treasure her (verse 22)?

4. Reflect on how well you're doing leaving your mother and father, uniting with your wife, and becoming one flesh with her? (See Genesis 2:24.) On a scale of 1 to 10 (1 = not so hot; 10 = fantastic), rate how you're doing in the following areas and write down one observation about your marriage in each area:

___ leaving (separating from family and friends in healthy ways, placing appropriate boundaries around your marriage)

___ uniting (becoming a soul mate with your wife)

___ becoming one flesh (pursuing intimacy with your wife)

Read Genesis 3:1-19.

5. What role did Satan play in causing friction between Adam and Eve?

6. What was Adam doing when chaos broke loose in the garden?

7. What was Adam responsible for, if anything? What should he have done differently?

8. What is the greatest cause of marital strife for you personally?

9. What evidence do you see in verse 12 that sin was having an impact on Adam and Eve's relationship?

10. In what ways do we mimic Adam in our own marital meltdowns? Why do we fail to accept responsibility for our own actions (verse 12)?

11. According to the last part of verse 16, why must the husband "rule over" (lead) his wife? (See 1 Corinthians 11:3.)

Connect with Group

Group Opener
Read the group opener aloud and discuss the questions that follow.

You may have heard it from your father often enough: "Real men take control of their homes." But real men aren't necessarily dictatorial leaders at home, as evidenced by Greg, one of the toughest guys you'll ever meet. On the football field, if you ran a crossing pattern at him, he'd split you in two and eat your liver as a party snack. A bright, tough farmer, Greg is part man and part beast, but he understands mutual submission and acts as a tender leader over his wife, Candy. Here's how she calls it:

> I am so fortunate to be Greg's wife. Each night when he comes
> home from work ready for a shower, he wants me to come
> into the bathroom to chat with him. That is so sweet, and
> I never thought God would grant me such a terrific mar-
> riage and husband, especially after all the creeps I dated in
> college.
>
>   Greg has four guys he meets with every Sunday night. A
> few don't have terrific marriages, but they know ours is some-

thing special. One of those men, speaking to Greg recently, said, "You must be doing something right because your wife obviously adores you." This made Greg feel great!

Many women have domineering husbands, but Greg considers my feelings every step of the way. Most of the time I find submission to Greg to be freeing because I know he seeks God first.

Hmm. Greg sounds manly to us. Anyone want to question the strength of his leadership?[4]

Discussion Questions

a. Talk about your view of Greg. In what ways are you like or unlike him?

b. Is Greg for real—or too good to be true? Explain.

c. List some reasons why men don't lead in the home.

---

4. Stephen Arterburn and Fred Stoeker, *Every Woman's Desire* (Colorado Springs: WaterBrook Press, 2001), 87-8.

d. Based on the passages in Genesis that we've just studied, what aspects of God's original plan for marriage have we lost?

e. What can we do to begin to see our wives as our helpers (2:18)?

f. What do you think would happen in your own marriage if you were to trust your wife's voice in your life a bit more? (See Proverbs 31:11-12.)

Standing Strong

What aspect of God's original plan for marriage do you plan to work on this week? What will you do? Be specific.

serve her

Demonstrate God's Love Toward Your Wife

Key Verse

Husbands, in the same way be considerate as you live with your wives, and treat them with respect as the weaker partner and as heirs with you of the gracious gift of life, so that nothing will hinder your prayers. (1 Peter 3:7)

Goals for Growth

- Recognize how our relationships with our wives affect the atmosphere in our homes.
- Realize how we have helped create this atmosphere.
- Commit to loving and caring for our wives in order to influence the entire family.

Head Start

Did you know that we men create the atmosphere for change in our homes? The way we treat our wives sets the tone of our family environment. When we are angry and controlling, we shut down our wives and children, effectively squelching their freedom to be themselves. When we are passive and detached, we distance ourselves from them, and they distance themselves from us. It all starts with the way we treat our wives. How do you view your wife? Is she merely the cook, cleaning lady, and chauffeur? Or is she the woman of your heart who's treated with care and respect?

When I (Todd) was dating Denise, she often reminded me that her dad wanted her to marry a man who would treat her like a queen. Well, I haven't always lived up to that expectation. When our girls were young, I quickly discovered that the way I treated my wife modeled the kind of behavior that was "acceptable" in our home. Unfortunately, the example I set wasn't always good. It took me a few years to realize that I need to defend Mom. She needs me to respect her and affirm her. Doing this not only makes her more attracted to me, but it also holds an eternal reward—a "well done, good and faithful servant" from God (Matthew 25:21).

Steve Farrar, author of *Point Man,* laid it on the line at a conference on marriage and divorce when he declared, "Men and women, I'll tell you what will cause the decline of divorce in America. It will only happen if husbands assume their God-given role as leaders of their homes and love their wives in an understanding way." That was not the answer everyone was hoping to hear. But it's the right one.

First Peter 3:1-7 teaches that the wife is to be submissive to the husband, but don't miss seeing who this passage was addressed to: the men of the church. They were responsible for creating an atmosphere for change in their homes. That means you and I have a responsibility to create an environment that enables our wives to follow our lead and encourages them to develop godly character. Being the spiritual leader is all about serving the needs of our wives. Our objective is clear.

Connect with the Word

Read 1 Peter 3:1-7.

1. Read this passage as though it were written directly to you. Based on what you have read, what can you do to bring about lasting change in your marriage?

2. Identify four qualities of a spiritual leader in this passage. (*Note:* Remember that even though Peter was instructing wives, he was also indirectly teaching husbands how to lead.)

3. What can you do to foster the kind of environment that will enable your wife to submit to your leadership (verses 1 and 2)?

4. What can you do to help your wife feel good about her inner qualities? In what ways can you encourage her to develop godly character (verses 3 and 6)?

5. How do you live with your wife "in an understanding way" (verse 7, NASB)?

6. In what ways do you show your wife honor (verse 7, NASB)?

Read Song of Songs 4:1,3,7,9-10; 7:5-6.

7. What do you learn from these passages about how to make your wife feel cherished? What specifically would you like to improve upon in this area?

Connect with the Group

Group Opener
Read the group opener aloud and discuss the questions that follow.

Author Fred Stoeker offers this view on marriage:

> Marriage is just a ridiculous concept, that's all. First, we take a male and female and tell them to become one. This alone is preposterous, considering the vast differences between men who are from Mars and women who are from Venus. Then throw in a host of other differences, such as temperaments, family environments, and religious backgrounds. After that, place them in a melting-pot culture inundated with sexual

images and warped by no-fault divorce with little social stigma. Grant the blushing couple a kiss for luck, pronounce them man and wife, and boot them into the great unknown through a hail of rice and a mountain of gifts. As they disappear around the corner in blissful ignorance, snort with a wink and a hearty chuckle, "The fun's just beginning! They don't even see it coming!"

I certainly didn't see the train coming my direction. Brenda and I never fought before the wedding, and we even liked the same pizza—Canadian bacon and pineapple. Surely our marriage was a match made in heaven. Yet on one lovely September evening the chiming of wedding bells faded quickly in the din of a terrible row between us.

We had stopped by her mother's house after the wedding reception to pick up a few things. Suddenly, the reality hit Brenda that she was really leaving home—for good. She couldn't tear herself away. As for me, I had been celibate for a year, and I was anxious to, well, you know, get moving to the honeymoon suite reserved for us at a nearby hotel. I certainly didn't want to hang around my mother-in-law's house sharing soup and crackers.

Two hours later, moments after I had finally carried Brenda over the threshold, I was steaming. Brenda had announced that she'd forgotten a bag. "We have to run home and get it," she said.

I flipped out. "Then you'll go without me!" I violently rifled a hairbrush across the hotel room.

After that inauspicious beginning, we got up the next morning and drove westbound toward Des Moines to begin our honeymoon.[5]

Discussion Questions

a. Can you relate to Fred's experience of the first days of marriage? Talk about your honeymoon experience in terms of the relational dynamics that occurred (but leave out the sex part!).

b. Compared to the honeymoon period, how easy or hard is it to love your wife these days? What are the differences between then and now?

---

5. Stephen Arterburn and Fred Stoeker, *Every Woman's Desire* (Colorado Springs: WaterBrook Press, 2001), 63-4.

c. List some of the reasons why we fail to understand and honor our wives after the wedding bliss has faded?

d. What connection do you find between verses 1-6 and verse 7 of 1 Peter 3?

e. What role can we play in helping our wives be submissive? What can we do to help them develop a positive self-image?

f. In what ways are women "weaker" than men (1 Peter 3:7)? What impact do these differences have on the way we understand our wives?

g. In the most practical terms, what can we do to show our w
honor day by day?

Standing Strong

What can you do this week to either understand your wife better or
honor her more? Be specific. Write your ideas below and share them
with the group.

love them

Connect with Your Kids

Key Verses

Sons are a heritage from the LORD, children a reward from him. (Psalm 127:3)

Then Esau looked up and saw the women and children. "Who are these with you?" he asked.

Jacob answered, "They are the children God has graciously given your servant." (Genesis 33:5)

Goals for Growth

- Recognize that fatherhood is a sacred trust.
- Identify God's priorities for fathers.
- Commit to connecting spiritually with our kids.

Head Start

It's been said that men spell intimacy S-E-X, women spell intimacy T-A-L-K, and kids spell intimacy T-I-M-E. When it comes right down to it, children would accept 80 percent less talk about love for the same amount of action in the form of time spent. Deep down they crave presence over presents. And presence is more than being together in the same space; it's about being into our kids. And remember: Whether you are great at spending time with your kids or are just giving them the crumbs of your busy life, they desire fellowship with Dad so much that they are forgiving to a fault.

God's plan for fathers is to "do" life together with their kids. That's the language kids speak. It's only by doing life together and spending time in their domains that we earn the right to teach them things about life.

If a dad is not spending meaningful time with his kids, a serious credibility gap develops. In fact, we find that the most common error fathers make with their children is *expecting respect without relationship.* Children might live with this contradiction for many years, but their hearts have a breaking point. At that point, they see our insecurities and failings clearly, they get tired of all our talk, and they lose hope. Inevitably, as author Josh McDowell so powerfully pointed out, "Rules without relationship leads to rebellion."

Kids are rebelling today because they need more than our time; they need us to understand them. Specifically, this means that we must be careful not to confuse postmodern youth culture with individual rebellion. Don't you remember the fads of your day? Were any of you low riders? We must get to know our kids in the culture in which they live. If we seek to understand them, our chances of instilling biblical and family values are much higher. The goal is inward spiritual formation, not outward conformity.

In the Bible, children are described as custom-wrapped gifts from God to us (see Psalm 127:3, NASB). They are to be opened, explored, integrated into our lives, and enjoyed. But make no mistake! Satan hates that we were given those diamonds in diapers; in fact, his goal is to divert our time and attention away from them. Through the guise of work and other "necessary" activities, he convinces us that we have to hurry through life. We have to hurry to get to work, to get the kids to school, to get the kids to soccer practice, to get the kids to finish their homework, to keep the kids occupied, and to put them to bed.

Why does Satan want us to be in a hurry? Because hurrying guarantees superficiality in our relationships. And when we have a superficial relationship with our kids, they won't respect our opinions, be open to our wisdom, or respond to our warnings when they need to the most.

In other words, fatherhood is a battlefield of spiritual warfare as well as a treasure of spiritual riches. So learn to fight effectively against your Enemy. Recognize that positively influencing our children requires our time. It also requires that we patiently pass on to them a healthy respect for God's will in their lives.

Connect with the Word

Read Mark 10:13-16.

1. Why do you think the disciples felt that children were not worth Jesus' time?

2. What did Jesus' response communicate to the disciples—and to everyone present (verse 14)?

3. According to Jesus, who benefits the most from entering into the world of a child and taking the time to be with him or her? What are some of the benefits?

4. What do Jesus' actions in verse 16 tell us about what children need?

5. What does this passage say to those whom God has seen fit to bless with children?

Read Ephesians 5:15-16.

6. What is the central theme of this passage?

7. How do you think verse 16 applies to fathers?

8. What compelling reason did Paul give for making the most of every opportunity?

Read Ephesians 6:1-4.

9. What is God's will for children in a family (verses 1 and 2)?

10. What does God promise them if they keep this command?

11. Why does God warn fathers not to exasperate (to irritate, annoy, anger) their children (verse 4)? What are the long-term consequences of doing this?

12. How does understanding the times in which we are living protect us from frustrating or exasperating our children?

Connect with the Group

Group Opener
Talk about some of the positive spiritual experiences you have had with your kids. Where were you? What were you doing? What happened? (If possible, talk about a time when the father-child relationship was excellent—or not so good.)

Discussion Questions

a. Based on Mark 10:13-16, in what ways do we behave like the disciples did when it comes to our kids? What message do our actions send to them?

b. What hard decisions and tough steps does it take to become the father your kids need? the father God wants you to be?

c. On a scale of 1 to 10 (1 = zero/none; 2-9 = some; 10 = a lot), how would *your children* rate you in the two main areas discussed in this session? Share your ratings with the group.

_____Time connecting with me when Dad's home.

_____Spiritual instruction and training from Dad.

d. In what ways might you be exasperating or discouraging your children?

e. In what ways are you "bring[ing] your children up in the training and instruction of the Lord" (Ephesians 6:4)?

f. Do you feel adequately equipped to lead your children spiritually? What steps do you need to take to ensure that you are equipped?

Standing Strong

In light of what you've learned in this week's session about being a godly father, what specific actions do you sense God leading you to take in the following areas? Share your list with the group.

Spending time with your kids:

Seeking to understand your kids' culture:

What do you want your legacy as a father to be? In the space provided, write a prayer to God expressing your desire.

have fun

Let the Good Times Roll!

Key Verse

I know that there is nothing better for men than to be happy and do good while they live. (Ecclesiastes 3:12)

Goals for Growth

- Evaluate the "fun quotient" in our families.
- Consider what an abundant family life would be like.
- Make our homes safe and fun places for children.

Head Start

Families need to have fun together. My (Todd's) greatest childhood memories involve times when my family and I went snow skiing in Mammoth or water-skiing at Lake Havasu or Lake Powell. Our family always took time to have fun. Today as adults with families of our own, we still take time to have fun. In fact, some of my closest friends in this world are my brother, my two sisters, and my folks. We still have a blast together. It's all because we value spending time together. The same is true of my wife's family. We thoroughly enjoy the time we spend with them as well. And in today's world, getting along with your own parents and siblings as well as your in-laws is nothing short of amazing, so we feel really blessed.

It takes a lot of planning to have fun as a family. There are so many distractions: television, e-mail, the phone, and a multitude of personal pursuits. But these distractions don't register with my son, Brandon. He simply loves family fun night. He can't wait for it. And it doesn't take anything spectacular to float his boat. He just likes connecting with Mom and Dad and his sisters. I want him to have those memories. And I feel fortunate because some families don't take the time to connect and enjoy one another.

The point is: If we as men don't create an atmosphere of fun for our families, the world will. Our kids will find other places and activities that give them pleasure. My wife has often said, "I want our house to be a fun and safe refuge from the world." That is, we want our kids to *want* to be in our home. We want them to bring their friends over and hang out. In fact, we'd rather have them in our house than in someone else's. Why? Because we don't know what's going on down the street. So we work hard to create the kind of home environment that makes our kids want to stick around.

At the same time, though, we know that kids can get into some serious trouble in their own homes if parents don't keep track of what's going on. A recent study revealed that most teenagers who lose their virginity do so in their own homes while their parents are there. Did that get your attention? So, what is going on in your home? Are you making it a fun, safe, and engaging place for your family!

Connect with the Word

Read John 10:10.

1. What does the abundant life look like as it relates to the family?

Read Psalm 16:11.

2. How does God's presence in your life affect your joy factor? Explain.

Read Nehemiah 8:10,12.

3. How does your enjoyment of God give you strength for living? How does this translate to your family?

Read Ecclesiastes 3:9-13.

4. In what ways does knowing the source of life as well as your eternal destiny enable you to enjoy your life?

5. List some practical ways you could begin enjoying life more fully as a family?

Connect with the Group

Group Opener
Read the group opener aloud and discuss the questions that follow.

Men often feel they have the authority to make these child-rearing decisions alone. We don't. The terms of oneness must constrain our rights. Listen to Susie as she shares this story:

> When my son Jimmie was three years old, I came home late one evening after running errands and purchasing a trunk-load

of groceries at Albertson's. My son rushed to the door to greet me and to tell me all about the movie *Rambo.* He had spent the previous two hours with his father (my husband, Rick) watching Sylvester Stallone shoot up people.

I frowned. Then the next week I came home from errands to learn that Jimmie had been watching *Die Hard.* A few months later, Rick asked me point-blank why Jimmie clearly had a problem with violence! Then he blamed me because I had let him watch *Peter Pan.*

Hello? Rick was giving me a hard time about *Peter Pan* and he was letting Jimmie watch these violent R-rated movies? I overheard Rick tell Jimmie, "It doesn't matter what you watch because it has no effect on your relationship with God."

Becoming nine years old turned out to be a particularly hard time for Jimmie. Sometimes in tears, he would tell me how he struggles "to be good, but it is very hard to be a Christian with Dad, because he wants me to watch television with him, and it's always the stuff you don't like, Mom. He always gets mad at me if I won't watch these shows with him."

Rick, for his part, would tease him and pressure him to "be normal." If I ask Rick about these things, he simply makes it harder on Jimmie the next time they are alone together. With Jimmie on the brink of adolescence, I'm finding it harder and harder for him to follow my rules, especially because Rick doesn't have any.

Clearly, Rick doesn't believe that watching violent R-rated movies is harmful to his own Christian belief system. He feels that he has the right to set his spiritual standard anywhere he chooses to set it.[6]

Discussion Questions

a. Put yourself in Rick's shoes. What is he thinking and feeling? What would you say to defend his actions?

b. Imagine being Rick's wife, Susie, for a moment. What is she thinking and feeling? Make her case in your own words.

c. Be little Jimmie. What is happening inside him? In a simple sentence, sum up what Jimmie really wants.

---

6. Stephen Arterburn and Fred Stoeker, *Every Woman's Desire* (Colorado Springs: WaterBrook Press, 2001), 215-6.

d. Describe one of your best family memories or experiences.

e. Why don't we naturally connect Jesus' promise of the abundant life to having fun with our families? Did Jesus intend the abundant life to be all about rules? If not, then what did He mean? How does it relate to life in your family?

f. How can your family become an Ecclesiastes kind of family? Be specific and practical!

Standing Strong

Write out how much time you spend each week in the following activities:

Working:

Commuting:

Participating in church and church-related activities:

Playing sports and working out:

Hanging out at home:

Watching television:

Talking or playing with the kids:

Talking on the phone with your grown kids:

Interacting with your wife:

Spending family time away from home:

What steps can you take to create more space in your schedule for quality time with your family?

Name one thing you will implement in your home this week to make it more fun for the kids.

work it out

Fight Fairly in Your Home

Key Verse

Do not let any unwholesome talk come out of your mouths, but only what is helpful for building others up according to their needs, that it may benefit those who listen. (Ephesians 4:29)

Goals for Growth

- Consider the role that fighting plays in our families and whether our fights are fair or unfair.
- Commit to fighting fairly to resolve conflicts in our families.
- Take the apostle Paul's advice about handling conflict—and apply his rules to our home lives.

Head Start

All families fight. Some fight fairly, others don't. What makes the difference? The fair fighters experience a more stable and loving home. They have learned not to punch below the belt.

In Ephesians 4:25-32, the apostle Paul lays out some very clear guidelines for quarreling in our homes. My wife and I (Todd) have used this passage for years to teach married couples how to fight fairly. We have tried to practice each and every one of these principles. (One of these days, we'll practice all of them during the same fight. I'm sure it will make a world of difference!)

Conflict is inevitable, yet how we work through it will determine the kind of marriage and family life we will have. Years ago an article in the *Los Angeles Times* revealed that a large percentage of murders take place in the home and are committed by a relative or family member. Billy Graham even said—with his wife standing right next to him—that in all the years they've been married, Ruth never considered divorce an option. But she did, on occasion, contemplate murder! Actually, that's not far from the truth for some couples.

Fighting is universal, but the wrong kind of fighting can destroy families. Like termites that eat away at the structure of the home, every fight gone awry gnaws away at our families. Kids go hide in their rooms and cover their ears, or worse, they leave home as soon as they can. *Why stick around if it's going to be like this?*

It's critical that we commit to working through the issues and problems our families face. Sadly, many Christians decide that family problems are just too difficult to resolve, so they abandon ship and instead seek to fill the void through their church family. God has indeed provided Christians with a church family to love and encourage them and to challenge them in their walk with Him, but God never intended the church to be a substitute for our families. If we can't learn to love and fight fairly with the natural families God gave us, then how can we expect to do it right in our church families?

The apostle Paul gives us some effective rules of engagement. Take a look. Learn from him. His guidelines work.

Connect with the Word

Read Ephesians 4:25-32.

1. How does lying break down our ability to work through conflict in our marriages?

2. What role does anger play in cutting off communication?

3. In what ways do we steal in the context of a relationship?

4. Why are our words so important, especially during conflict?

5. Why do you think Paul did not place any conditions on forgiveness? What can get in the way of forgiveness (verse 31)?

6. Spend a few minutes thinking about your own home. Which of Paul's guidelines are you applying? Which are you ignoring? Write down some thoughts about the home environment you are creating by the way you work through your arguments.

Connect with the Group

Group Opener
Read the group opener aloud and discuss the questions that follow.

Recently, my wife and I (Todd) refinanced our home. I had arranged to be home by 4:00 P.M. that day to sign loan documents that the title officer planned to bring by our house. My wife also agreed to be home at that time.

Unfortunately, things got busy at work, and I couldn't break loose. I called the title officer and asked him to swing by my office so I could sign the papers before he headed to my house so my wife could sign them. What I didn't realize was how long it takes to sign loan papers. As I began signing page after page, I realized there was no way I could finish in time for him to get to our house by four o'clock.

I was in big trouble.

I called my wife, but I couldn't reach her. About five o'clock, she called my office. "The guy isn't here yet."

Silence. "I know," I said. "He's here with me."

"That means I can't leave the house until he gets here, and I have to run an errand before I leave for an evening party I'm attending," Denise said. "What are you thinking?"

I calmly said, "Did you get my message?"

She hadn't—and she was hot. At that moment I felt *my* blood boil too. *I couldn't help that I wasn't able to get home to sign the papers! I thought. I got busy. After all, I have to work for a living. Cut me some slack! You can sit tight for another hour.* I wanted to pounce all over my wife for being upset with me. I wanted to defend myself as I have so many times in the past. But for some reason I came to my senses before I said another word. Instead, I apologized. I didn't defend myself. I didn't speak and dig myself a deeper hole.

You know what? That conflict ended pretty well. We both survived. I kept my cool, watched my words, and honestly admitted my part in the problem. It worked out.

Discussion Questions

a. What percentage of the arguments with your wife are over big, irreconcilable, marriage-collapsing issues? Does your answer surprise you? Explain.

b. What lies do men tend to tell their wives?

c. What family issues seem to ignite your anger most easily?

d. How does laziness in our marital relationships contribute to conflict in the home?

e. What is the difference between words that tear down and words that build up? Give an example.

f. What's holding you back from forgiving your spouse for something she has done that hurt you? (*Note:* Share only what you can without exposing your wife's faults in front of the group.)

g. How can a man follow the guidelines of decency presented in Ephesians 4 and still work through conflict? Explain.

Standing Strong

Of the negative behaviors described in today's Scripture passage, which do you tend to repeat during a conflict? What can you do to prevent this from happening the next time?

What specific steps can you take to turn down the steam and turn up the communication during a quarrel with your wife?

The next time you have an argument with your wife, ask yourself the following questions:

- What's really the issue here?
- What part do I need to own?
- How does my wife feel right now?
- How do I feel right now?

pour it on

Foster Spiritual Connections

Key Verse

Love the LORD your God with all your heart and with all your soul and with all your strength. These commandments that I give you today are to be upon your hearts. Impress them on your children. Talk about them when you sit at home and when you walk along the road, when you lie down and when you get up. (Deuteronomy 6:5-7)

Goals for Growth

- Recognize that fathers are God-appointed ambassadors to the family.
- Loyally represent God in our words and actions to our families.
- Establish specific family activities for the purpose of increasing spiritual maturity.

Head Start

As I (Kenny) stood behind three other sets of parents, waiting to introduce myself to my son's second-grade teacher, I thought I was wasting my time. I mean, really, what was she going to tell me about Ryan that I didn't already know? Finally, the mom in front of me finished her conversation, and it was my turn.

"Hello, I am Ryan's dad."

"Hello, I am Mrs. Dubay."

"So, how's Ryan doing in your class?"

"Ryan is the shining light in the class."

For a few seconds I was speechless. Not because I was in shock at her statement (he's a pretty good kid), but because of the prayers Ryan and I had been offering to God at bedtime in the days preceding back-to-school night. In our family I put the kids to bed every night I'm home. Ryan is a stickler. He simply will not go to sleep without my praying for him.

The night before he started second grade, I knelt down next to his bed and grabbed the first decent sounding thought that fit the occasion. We talked for a little bit, and then I said, "Let's pray." I asked God to make Ryan "a light to his teacher and his friends at school through his words, through good listening, and through kindness to others." We had prayed this way each night leading up to back-to-school night. Now perhaps you can understand why Mrs. Dubay caught me a little off-guard.

When I got home, Ryan was waiting for me. I put on my best poker face and said, "Guess what the first words out of Mrs. Dubay's mouth were?" When I told him what she'd said, it was as if a ten-megaton joy-bomb had exploded in his heart. I watched the words travel from my mouth into his mind and sink deep into his heart, producing a coast-to-coast grin (and a subsequent hug).

It was clear to us both that God had answered our specific petition for Ryan. And we both, as father and son, experienced the joy of God's answer.

So many nights I walk away from the kids' bedsides wondering if I am putting them to sleep or if I sound like Charlie Brown's parents—unintelligible. God wanted to let Ryan know that He is living and real and listening to him. So He decided to show up where I least expected Him. The key was doing what only I could do in order to allow God to do what only He could do. In this session, we'll explore the ways God uses our initiative in fostering spiritual connections within our families to reveal His power and affirm His plan for our lives together.

Connect with the Word

Read Deuteronomy 6:5-25.

1. What do you think it means that God's priorities "are to be upon your hearts" (verse 6)?

2. Based on the picture presented in verse 7, how does a father "impress" God's priorities upon his children? How does that differ from your own interaction with your kids?

3. According to verse 8, to what lengths should we go to make sure that God is first in the minds of everyone in the family?

4. What are some practical ways your family can place God continually at the center of family life so that you don't forget Him or what He's done?

5. Reread verse 14. When does a man tend to do when he forgets God or assigns Him a lesser place in the family system? What impact does this have on his family?

6. Consider verses 20-25. When your son or daughter asks you the inevitable questions about life, what answer will you give? What testimony will you give about God's working in your life?

7. What reason is given in verse 24 for doing life God's way?

Connect with the Group

Group Opener

Describe a time, if any, when you have tended to relegate God to Sundays and other "spiritual" events rather than inviting Him into the daily life of your family.

Discussion Questions

a. What can we do to make knowing and following God part of our family lifestyle? Brainstorm a list of practical ideas with the group.

b. Based on Deuteronomy 6:15, what is the bottom-line consequence of failing to provide spiritual leadership to your family?

c. What are some of the "other gods" that husbands and fathers risk leading their families to follow or value over the Lord (verse 14)?

d. What are some of the lies Satan throws at us to keep us from fostering spiritual connections in our families?

e. How you lead is as important as leading itself. Read Philippians 2:1-8 aloud in the group. What example of leadership did Jesus give us to follow? With what result? What does leading a family Jesus' way involve?

Standing Strong

What is one spiritual connection you would like to foster in your family this week? Be specific (i.e., with whom? doing what? etc.). Share your plan with the group.

Plan a family devotion time this week:

Day of the week: _____

Time: _____

Activities:

    Prayer

    Bible reading (one passage)

    One discussion question

Questions for the family:

    How's your week going?

    What's one thing you're struggling with this week?

    What's one thing you're excited about this week?

Write a prayer in the space below, asking God to help you see and take advantage of future moments to represent Him to your family.

small-group resources

What if men aren't doing the Connect with the Word section before our small-group session?

Don't be discouraged. You set the pace. If you are doing the study and regularly referring to it in conversations with your men throughout the week, they will pick up on its importance. Here are some suggestions to motivate the men in your group to do their home Bible study:

- Send out a midweek e-mail in which you share your answer to one of the study questions. This shows them that you are personally committed to and involved in the study.
- Ask the guys to hit "respond to all" on their e-mail program and share one insight from that week's Bible study with the entire group. Encourage them to send it out before the next small-group session.
- Every time you meet, ask each man in the group to share one insight from his home study.

What if men are not showing up for small group?

This might mean they are losing a sin battle and don't want to admit it to the group. Or they might be consumed with other priorities. Or maybe they don't think they're getting anything out of the group. Here are some suggestions for getting the guys back each week:

- Affirm them when they show up, and tell them how much it means to you that they make small group a priority.

- From time to time, ask them to share one reason they think small group is important to them.
- Regularly call or send out an e-mail the day before you meet to remind them you're looking forward to seeing them.
- Check in with any guy who has missed more than one session, and find out what's going on in his life.
- Get some feedback from the men. You may need to adjust your style. Listen and learn.

What if group discussion is not happening?

You are a discussion facilitator. You have to keep guys involved in the discussion or you'll lose them. You can engage a man who isn't sharing by saying, "Chuck, you've been quiet. What do you think about this question or discussion?" You should also be prepared to share your own personal stories that are related to the discussion questions. You'll set the example by the kind of sharing you do.

What if one man is dominating the group time?

You have to deal with it. If you don't, men will stop showing up. No one wants to hear from just one guy all the time. It will quickly kill morale. Meet with the guy in person and privately. Firmly but gently suggest that he allow others more time to talk. Be positive and encouraging, but truthful. You might say, "Bob, I notice how enthusiastic you are about the group and how you're always prepared to share your thoughts with the group. But there are some pretty quiet guys in the group too. Have you noticed? Would you be willing to help me get them involved in speaking up?"

How do I get the guys in my group more involved?

Give them something to do. Ask one guy to bring a snack. Invite another to lead the prayer time (ask in advance). Have one guy sub for you one week as the leader. (Meet with him beforehand to walk through the group program and the time allotments for each segment.) Encourage another guy to lead a subgroup.

What if guys are not being vulnerable during the Standing Strong or prayer times?

You model openness. You set the pace. Honesty breeds honesty. Vulnerability breeds vulnerability. Are you being vulnerable and honest about your own problems and struggles? (This doesn't mean that you have to spill your guts each week or reveal every secret of your life.) Remember, men want an honest, on-their-level leader who strives to walk with God. (Also, as the leader, you need an accountability partner, perhaps another group leader.)

What will we do at the first session?

We encourage you to open by discussing the **Small-Group Covenant** we've included in this resource section. Ask the men to commit to the study, and then discuss how long it will take your group to complete each session. (We suggest 75-90 minute sessions.) Men find it harder to come up with excuses for missing a group session if they have made a covenant to the other men right at the start.

Begin to identify ways certain men can play a more active role in small group. Give away responsibility. You won't feel as burdened, and your men will grow from the experience. Keep in mind that this process can take a few weeks. Challenge men to fulfill one of the group roles identified later in this resource section. If no one steps forward to fill a role, say to one of the men, "George, I've noticed that you are comfortable praying in a group. Would you lead us each week during that time?"

How can we keep the group connected after we finish a study?
Begin talking about starting another Bible study before you finish this eight-week study. (There are six studies to choose from in the Every Man Bible study series.) Consider having a social time at the conclusion of the study, and encourage the men to invite a friend. This will help create momentum and encourage growth as you launch into another study with your group. There are probably many men in your church or neighborhood who aren't in small groups but would like to be. Be the kind of group that includes others.

As your group grows, consider choosing an apprentice leader who can take half the group into another room for the **Connect with the Group** time. That subgroup can stay together for prayer, or you can reconvene as a large group during that time. You could also meet for discussion as a large group, and then break into subgroups for **Standing Strong** and **prayer.**

If your group doubles in size, it might be a perfect opportunity to release your apprentice leader with half the group to start another group. Allow men to pray about this and make a decision as a group. Typically, the relational complexities that come into play when a small group births a new group work themselves out. Allow guys to choose which group they'd like to be a part of. If guys are slow in choosing one group or another, ask them individually to select one of the groups. Take the lead in making this happen.

Look for opportunities for your group to serve in the church or community. Consider a local outreach project or a short-term missions trip. There are literally hundreds of practical ways you can serve the Lord in outreach. Check with your church leaders to learn the needs in your congregation or community. Create some interest by sending out scouts who will return with a report for the group. Serving keeps men from becoming self-focused and ingrown. When you serve as a group, you will grow as a group.

using this study in a large-group format

Many church leaders are looking for biblically based curriculum that can be used in a large-group setting, such as a Sunday-school class, or for small groups within an existing larger men's group. Each of the Every Man Bible studies can be adapted for this purpose. In addition, this curriculum can become a catalyst for churches wishing to launch men's small groups or to build a men's ministry in their church.

Getting Started

Begin by getting the word out to men in your church, inviting them to join you for a men's study based on one of the topics in the Every Man Bible study series. You can place a notice in your church bulletin, have the pastor announce it from the pulpit, or pursue some other means of attracting interest.

Orientation Week

Arrange your room with round tables and chairs. Put approximately six chairs at each table.

Start your class in prayer and introduce your topic with a short but motivational message from any of the scriptures used in the Bible study. Hand out the curriculum and challenge the men to do their homework before each class. During this first session give the men some discussion questions based upon an overview of the material and have them talk things through just within their small group around the table.

Just before you wrap things up, have each group select a table host or leader. You can do this by having everyone point at once to the person at their table they feel would best facilitate discussion for future meetings.

Ask those newly elected table leaders to stay after for a few minutes, and offer them an opportunity to be further trained as small-group leaders as they lead discussions throughout the course of the study.

Subsequent Weeks

Begin in prayer. Then give a short message (15-25 minutes) based upon the scripture used for that lesson. Pull out the most motivating topics or points and strive to make the discussion relevant to the life of an everyday man and his world. Then leave time for each table to work through the discussion questions listed in the curriculum. Be sure the discussion facilitators at each table close in prayer.

At the end of the eight sessions, you might want to challenge each "table group" to become a small group, inviting them to meet regularly with their new small-group leader and continue building the relationships they've begun.

prayer request record

Date:
Name:
Prayer Request:
Praise:

Date:
Name:
Prayer Request:
Praise:

Date:
Name:
Prayer Request:
Praise:

Date:
Name:
Prayer Request:
Praise:

Date:
Name:
Prayer Request:
Praise:

defining group roles

Group Leader: Leads the lesson and facilitates group discussion.

Apprentice Leader: Assists the leader as needed, which may include leading the lesson.

Refreshment Coordinator: Maintains a list of who will provide refreshments. Calls group members on the list to remind them to bring what they signed up for.

Prayer Warrior: Serves as the contact person for prayer between sessions. Establishes a list of those willing to pray for needs that arise. Maintains the prayer-chain list and activates the chain as needed by calling the first person on the list.

Social Chairman: Plans any desired social events during group sessions or at another scheduled time. Gathers members for planning committees as needed.

small-group roster

Name:
Address:
Phone: E-mail:

Name:
Address:
Phone: E-mail:

Name:
Address:
Phone: E-mail:

Name:
Address:
Phone: E-mail:

Name:
Address:
Phone: E-mail:

Name:
Address:
Phone: E-mail:

spiritual checkup

Your answers to the statements below will help you determine which areas you need to work on in order to grow spiritually. Mark the appropriate letter to the left of each statement. Then make a plan to take one step toward further growth in each area. Don't forget to pray for the Lord's wisdom before you begin. Be honest. Don't be overly critical or rationalize your weaknesses.

Y = Yes
S = Somewhat or Sometimes
N = No

My Spiritual Connection with Other Believers

____I am developing relationships with Christian friends.

____I have joined a small group.

____I am dealing with conflict in a biblical manner.

____I have become more loving and forgiving than I was a year ago.

____I am a loving and devoted husband and father.

My Spiritual Growth

____I have committed to daily Bible reading and prayer.

____I am journaling on a regular basis, recording my spiritual growth.

____I am growing spiritually by studying the Bible with others.

____I am honoring God in my finances and personal giving.

____I am filled with joy and gratitude for my life, even during trials.

____I respond to challenges with peace and faith instead of anxiety and anger.

____I avoid addictive behaviors (excessive drinking, overeating, watching too much TV, etc.).

Serving Christ and Others

____I am in the process of discovering my spiritual gifts and talents.

____I am involved in ministry in my church.

____I have taken on a role or responsibility in my small group.

____I am committed to helping someone else grow in his spiritual walk.

Sharing Christ with Others

____I care about and am praying for those around me who are unbelievers.

____I share my experience of coming to know Christ with others.

____I invite others to join me in this group or for weekend worship services.

____I am seeing others come to Christ and am praying for this to happen.

____I do what I can to show kindness to people who don't know Christ.

Surrendering My Life for Growth

___I attend church services weekly.

___I pray for others to know Christ, and I seek to fulfill the Great Commission.

___I regularly worship God through prayer, praise, and music, both at church and at home.

___I care for my body through exercise, nutrition, and rest.

___I am concerned about using my energy to serve God's purposes instead of my own.

My Identity in the Lord

___I see myself as a beloved son of God, one whom God loves regardless of my sin.

___I can come to God in all of my humanity and know that He accepts me completely. When I fail, I willingly run to God for forgiveness.

___I experience Jesus as an encouraging Friend and Lord each moment of the day.

___I have an abiding sense that God is on my side. I am aware of His gracious presence with me throughout the day.

___During moments of beauty, grace, and human connection, I lift up praise and thanks to God.

___I believe that using my talents to their fullest pleases the Lord.

___I experience God's love for me in powerful ways.

small-group covenant

As a committed group member, I agree to the following:*

- **Regular Attendance.** I will attend group sessions on time and let everyone know in advance if I can't make it.
- **Group Safety.** I will help create a safe, encouraging environment where men can share their thoughts and feelings without fear of embarrassment or rejection. I will not judge another guy or attempt to fix his problems.
- **Confidentiality.** I will always keep to myself everything that is shared in the group.
- **Acceptance.** I will respect different opinions or beliefs and let Scripture be the teacher.
- **Accountability.** I will make myself accountable to the other group members for the personal goals I share.
- **Friendliness.** I will look for those around me who might join the group and explore their faith with other men.
- **Ownership.** I will prayerfully consider taking on a specific role within the group as the opportunity arises.
- **Spiritual Growth.** I will commit to establishing a daily quiet time with God, which includes doing the homework for this study. I will share with the group the progress I make and the struggles I experience as I seek to grow spiritually.

Signed: _____ Date: _____

---

*   *Permission is given to photocopy and distribute this form to each man in your group. Review this covenant quarterly or as needed.*

about the authors

STEPHEN ARTERBURN is coauthor of the best-selling Every Man series. He is also founder and chairman of New Life Clinics, host of the daily *New Life Live!* national radio program, and creator of the Women of Faith conferences. A nationally known speaker and licensed minister, Stephen has authored more than forty books. He lives with his family in Laguna Beach, California.

KENNY LUCK is president and founder of Every Man Ministries and coauthor of *Every Man, God's Man* and its companion workbook. He is division leader for men's small groups and teaches a men's interactive Bible study at Saddleback Church in Lake Forest, California. He and his wife, Chrissy, have three children and reside in Rancho Santa Margarita, California.

TODD WENDORFF is a graduate of U.C. Berkeley and holds a Th.M. from Talbot School of Theology. He serves as a pastor of men's ministries at Saddleback Church and is an adjunct professor at Biola University. He is an author of the Doing Life Together Bible study series. Todd and his wife, Denise, live with their three children in Trabuco Canyon, California.

every man's battle
workshops

from New Life Ministries

new Life Ministries receives hundreds of calls every month from Christian men who are struggling to stay pure in the midst of daily challenges to their sexual integrity and from pastors who are looking for guidance in how to keep fragile marriages from falling apart all around them.

As part of our commitment to equip individuals to win these battles, New Life Ministries has developed biblically based workshops directly geared to answer these needs. These workshops are held several times per year around the country.

- Our workshops **for men** are structured to equip men with the tools necessary to maintain sexual integrity and enjoy healthy, productive relationships.

- Our workshops **for church leaders** are targeted to help pastors and men's ministry leaders develop programs to help families being attacked by this destructive addiction.

Some comments from previous workshop attendees:

"An awesome, life-changing experience. Awesome teaching, teacher, content and program."   —DAVE

"God has truly worked a great work in me since the EMB workshop. I am fully confident that with God's help, I will be restored in my ministry position. Thank you for your concern. I realize that this is a battle, but I now have the weapons of warfare as mentioned in Ephesians 6:10, and I am using them to gain victory!"   —KEN

"It's great to have a workshop you can confidently recommend to anyone without hesitation, knowing that it is truly life changing. Your labors are not in vain!"   —DR. BRAD STENBERG, Pasadena, CA

If sexual temptation is threatening your marriage or your church, please call **1-800-NEW-LIFE** to speak with one of our specialists.

every man conferences
revolutionizing local churches

"This is a revolutionary conference that has the potential to change the world. Thanks Kenny! The fire is kindled!" —B.J.

"The conference was tremendous and exactly what I needed personally. The church I pastor is starting a men's group to study the material launched at this conference. This is truly an answer to my prayer!" —DAVID

"Thank you! Thank you! Thank you! I didn't know how much I needed this. I look forward to working through the material with my small group." —BOB

"It's the only conference I have attended where I will go back and read my notes!" —ROGER

"This is a conference every man should attend." —KARL

"After years of waffling with God, I am ready to welcome Him into my every day life. Thanks for giving me the tools to help me develop a relationship with God." —GEORGE

"This revolutionary conference is the next wave of men's ministry in America." —STEVE ARTERBURN, Coauthor of *Every Man's Battle*

If you want to :
- **address the highest felt need issues among men**
- **launch or grow your men's ministry**
- **connect your men in small groups around God's Word**
- **and reach seeking men with the Gospel**

Join with other churches or sponsor an every man conference in your area.

For information on booking Kenny Luck or scheduling an Every Man Conference contact Every Man Ministries at 949-766-7830 or email at everymanministries@aol.com. For more information on Every Man events, visit our website at everymanministries.com.

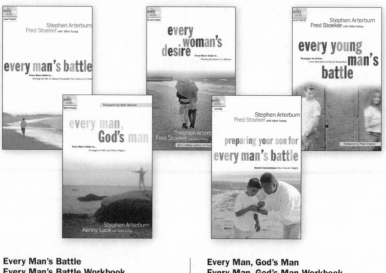